THE LIBRARY
ST. MARY'S COLLEGE OF MARYLAND
ST. MARY'S CITY, MARYLAND 20686

T5-BYU-759

THE
SECULARIST

THE
SECULARIST

POEMS BY

Claudia Keelan

The University of Georgia Press

Athens and London

Published by the University of Georgia Press
Athens, Georgia 30602
© 1997 by Claudia Keelan
All rights reserved
Designed by Betty Palmer McDaniel
Set in 10/13 Sabon
by Books International, Inc.
Printed and bound by McNaughton and Gunn, Inc.
The paper in this book meets the guidelines for
permanence and durability of the Committee on
Production Guidelines for Book Longevity of the
Council on Library Resources.

Printed in the United States of America

01 00 99 98 97   P   5 4 3 2 1

Library of Congress Cataloging in Publication Data
Keelan, Claudia, 1959–
The secularist : poems / by Claudia Keelan.
p.   cm. — (The contemporary poetry series)
ISBN 0-8203-1802-7 (pbk. : alk. paper)
I. Title.   II. Series: Contemporary poetry series
(University of Georgia Press)
PS3561.E3387S43   1997
811'.54—dc20   95-36584

British Library Cataloging in Publication Data available

To this world

ACKNOWLEDGMENTS

Agni: "While the Wind Speaks" (as "To My Teacher"),
   "Rushing the Gates of Empirical Gardens"
American Letters & Commentary: "The Secularist"
American Poetry Review: "And Its Discontents"
Antioch Review: "Fallout"
Black Warrior Review: "Parable 4," "Parable 4b," "Richter,"
   "Spring"
Boulevard: "The Camera's Eye Turned to You and Then the
   Beginning of Static"
Calliope: "Demography"
Caliban: "One Parable"
Columbia: "The Body You Love May Be Your Own"
Columbia Poetry Review: "Tractatus Française," "Chalktrace"
Denver Quarterly: "Free Verse," "The End Is an Animal"
Heaven Bone: "Bartók Window," "To Sleep"
Kentucky Writing: "Past Crossing," "An American Primitivist
   inside Her Painting"
New American Writing: "Parable 2," "Parable 6," "Same
   Question"
River Styx: "The Modern Life of the Soul," "Parable 5"
Volt: "Ave Verum Corpus" (as "Three")
Willow Springs: "Chaff"

Thanks go to the Kentucky Foundation for Women for a grant
that helped in the completion of this book.

CONTENTS

THE WORLD AS MEDIATION

TRANSPARENCY

THE
SECULARIST

THE SECULARIST

I know the staggering
    lights from the Hancock Tower
searing the river's face
    were the end of the story.

But in that light, stripped of candescence,
    sinking into the river's crawl,
I almost believed
    again, candle's flicker

spreading, in the underwater church,
    across the feet of the stewards,
across the money box
    where they dropped their love, across

the stone robes, and what we call *answers,*
    kept hidden there. In after
-thought: the light brushed finally
    the feet of the kind, dearly dead god.

I stood there often,
    fingering absence at the Charles'
edge. I considered
    my choices. There in that place

—what was it you called it?—
    "the spirit of matter"
raised its divining finger
    toward me. What do you do

with light you can't be quit
    of, throwing its gleam

on you from a holy grave
    you thought you'd dreamed

clear out of your sleep
    years ago? I'm trying to say
I didn't want that touch
    there in that imagined place,

couldn't want that touch
    here on the nearly ruined shore.
Behind me, in the real city,
    the coal muffles the birth
-cry of the woman

    cutting her own umbilici
in a single room. She wraps
    the slippery string around
the child's neck, kisses

it once on the forehead,
    and tightens. Do you hear
her prayers mumbled rapid
    fire? The spirit of matter

scratches its ass against
    a brick wall. I know
if I stay here
    let the light drift

slowly across me
    I could feel love.
But, I'm going to go home.
    I'm waking up in my own bed.

TO MY TEACHER

Most honors my style who learns under it to destroy the teacher . . .

WALT WHITMAN, "Song of Myself"

FREE VERSE

                                              I've been reading
the hieroglyphics of the new gangs
on the corner wall, but they're still
speaking in your tongue.
Derrick and Bad Boy be dying
in "good" blood, this whole city block
written in huge, unrecognizable print,
human figures sometimes, mostly empty
tracings and signs like swastikas
but not swastikas exactly, exaggerated o's
and mixed up letters all mouthing
honor of the late-century kind:
"This is not a war," on New Year's Eve
the news begins, rounds and rounds
of machine-gun fire in east
Los Angeles, filling my mother's kitchen.
    Who looketh for thee,
in the smoking Uzi air,
    speaketh not. In mortal
agony, fighting on thy terms,
    the vowels not uttered sing
from any listening room in the world.

SOMETHING TO KEEP

Because this began from love,
a whisper in passing, approval
lighting her hair. Here is where
my name steps in, *Claudia,*
from the Latin meaning
lame, calling come home   come home
I will hold us safely together,
we will consider the falling whole.
Cripple with an empire of days
attached to her body.
Do you know enough to say it
the parts ask, do you love
enough to reveal us, paper,
flesh, the face of the rain
on the microscope's slide,
your one good eye?
Nothing ever again free
from the collusion of my entry,
climbing the bus stair promising
to let it all wash over me,
swearing to let it all wash over me
so I may give it back, intact.
All the eddying qualities snarling
in the narrow aisle air,
if I can just be quiet,
not resist them,
let them wash over, not into, me
won't this be ours then?
Won't there be room then,
for my omissions,
his intention to kill,

her three bags of personal sorrow,
the driver's final, unspoken fear of his job?
I need to ask you now, teacher,
why it's destination you defy.
See, I'm on the bus regardless,
some kind of collage of coal and grief,
and sometimes a bird, or the wind,
threading *here* to that other *there*
makes me especially anxious to arrive.
Does the God we believe in want us,
howling and dirty from the listening?
How will I ask forgiveness now,
driving this packed bus
to the only where I know?

PAST CROSSING

There where things grow unbraided:
the river much too high, the crossing
    the idea of crossing to home,
vanishing. Meanwhile the car lots
    and churches, twenty unnamed dogs,
children dirty on sagging porches.
    A day you'd never risk knowing
if you met it edging up between the part
    ridden yards. So many
churches, did you know there'd be
so many churches, recorded bells
muttering against the rubble of hours.
    The fat lady peers out
of her minute-laden looking.
    I want to ask her what this is for,
what the doll's head and mattress
    are a part of, there in her sitting,
in my walking. Of course there's a secret
    in the field outside of town.
I've been there before, rung in
    by the wind's lack of restraint
across the lake's easy surface,
    but I want to know about her,
fat mother I feel no pity
    for, quietly surveying the ruin
she is part of. Something in her
    closes my lids each night,
and too afraid to pray, I dream
    the river's flood leaving
us irrevocably on this side,
    her lap, her lap reader, our bounty.

THE BODY YOU LOVE MAY BE YOUR OWN

                                        See, I could say I own this
but I'm looking at your prints all over
the place. How is it you never touch
the old couple I've been following
for thousands of miles, lolling poodle
bobbing its reverent canine head?
They do the best they can, driving
again and again into their own notion of arrival,
the sun a radioactive pink the trailer cannot but
glean to. I've tried to see their faces in the road's mirage
but the sun puts up a ferocious wagging.
Even on the subway I was drawn
by the sunlit, bored face of the Charles—
did I ever really want a part of that?
Here's one for the time spent in the tunnel,
in popcorn and coal, the calf in the box
peering out as the light shifts
its notion of veal intact.

WHO WILL NOT JOIN TOGETHER

Was it light?
Was it light within. . . ?
Stillness becoming alive
Yet Still?

THEODORE ROETHKE,
"The Lost Son"

An old man dragging a tree limb,
an old woman following slowly behind.
They are the first people,
the only steady arrangement of flesh
this day or you will know.
They take their time,
light digressing into slits
across the grass, the light sick
with calling *there's nothing to spare,*
nothing to save for,
an old man dragging a tree limb
an old woman following slowly behind.
They keep repeating,
working toward something
the light suggests
blinding near its end,
on the cars going home
for the day, playing itself out
on the bits of paper and rocks,
the pieces of wood and car parts,
the good family's neatly trimmed lawn.
Each thing it touches either
useful or not, to this looking,
lending its *function* to the light's
gradual playing out, or not,

an old man dragging a tree limb,
an old woman following slowly behind.
And it's better to keep working, isn't it,
despite the light's betrayal,
the plan it has outside you,
formulated in a place like a government
hall but not there exactly?
Don't you see it's a crony,
following some *other* motion's
orders, no blueprint of its own,
its order a randomness, its design
a trick not meant for us,
though we look often into its
indifferent center, into its warmth
splayed now on the sidewalk a cat
lies on. Apologetic, sorry,
but for the looking, the steady looking.

PAST TRAVEL

Past Locust Grove
Baptist Church, one mile,
the hay sprung and coiled
in a yellow field;
past the church itself,
the holy sitting stunned
as evening falls inside,
coins filling the straw
basket; beyond the grave
-yard, plastic roses
smelling sweet; over
the ridges and rough shoulders;
past a man burning
refuse on the boundary
of his lands, his boy walking
slowly toward him
in the sweet, gray smoke;
the burning refuse
the burning man
the burning boy
their shimmer
receding ever so slowly in my rear
-view mirror; rising past
travel, past the idea of travel;
into the air of some other
enormous and confined
changing colored thing;
past the four-way stop and through
realize you've gone
the wrong way

AN AMERICAN PRIMITIVIST
INSIDE HER PAINTING

The river I watch
moving unnamed today
is mud and water. Rain pocks its face.
Boats pass: *Ponyboy* and *King Fisher*.
Something's dead here,
something's asking to be remembered,
(though the far green
on the other side
seems serene). Kentucky,
"dark and bloody land,"
I come to you a stranger
with none of the stranger's shy respect.
Your river is beyond sorrow,
and the neighbor woman barely moving
in the part-ridden yard
seems some kind of obese icon
to defeat. In a pen,
three dogs keep their day.
The middle dog, the oldest, I think,
sometimes suddenly turns
to both sides of the fence,
snarling at her companions.
She bites the wire,
jumps first to one side
then the other, of the cage.
This afternoon,
her master will shoot the river,
his bullets licking its face.

WHILE THE WIND SPEAKS

All you have to do is try to keep it alive,
water in a manmade ditch with somewhere
to go. *Won't you get out of bed? Something*
out there needs you in it. All you have to do
is try to keep—But the succession of birds the cat
gets somehow by the neck—all we had to do was try to—
But the wild bled clean out of them, our misguided
hands washing the wound, putting on the salve.
It's not too deep, is it? It's not the wild
given up to will, is it? Because the wind blows through
the corn, right? Up and down each row and through
the corn, right? Until some days it's freedom itself
the corn won't allow. Until it's morning itself
we heard boxed in out there in the field. And the corn,
instrument of order, sorry when it's won, laying down
its tassel flags, etc. etc. etc.

                             Forgive me my day, my teacher.
I'm listening, but the beagle keeps crying now
that hunting season is over. Neighbor of mine the dark won't
let rest, bred to sniff out the waiting. O.K., little brother,
I hear you. *Over there.* But the chain-link fence.
Inside the cage, friend. Inside the cage, dig your pretty
face into the dirt.

THE NECESSARY ANGEL

Because I want to startle it
one decaying garden,
one stick, stone,
burning blade of grass,
at a time—

Standing there with its back turned.

Standing there with the big news,

crony of white light,
ridged wings too heavy with the words
of that other world
it is tired of speaking
for, the face that cannot ever
be seen—
Picked and labeled already
for the tentative green
it stands in, picked and labeled
already to live with us
in our separate fates, guardian
of the bridge children walk,
guardian as it collapses and falls—
Angel of suicide, infant death,
angel of good father,
bad father, unfinished girl
shot in a police raid oh
they are sick in it,
tendons of air their sex
too perfect to hold—they must
love you completely,
last figure tethered
in the now-green light,

(but where is your face)
feathers pulsing,
(but where is your face)
no hands to speak of,
(but where is your face)
gathering your thin blood
into it (have you ever woven
better?) And the birds
you can name, quiet in it—
yellowbelly, cardinal, cowbird,
no nest or where to go—
gathering your thin blood into it—
(but I want to see it now)
What do you see
(I cannot see)
What do you see
(Ants navigating a green vine
birdsong dog bark trapped
fat mother in a yard)
No you have to love it now
(But it didn't love me)
Love it
(The insects coming on
for the night, the blue
bug light)
Love it
The insects made of light
and no one calling
nothing finished as evening
tells, the myths given
back their names (what is the word
for lonely song)
the angel collecting me and we fall
(back down)
No, through.

ARMISTICE

The preflight of the sweet jets. The public dying down below.
I was left
a private woman, a discreet investigation.
How did I come to assume
the other's day? His walking against traffic, her upturned hand,
all the voices spilling hair
into my mouth while I slept? There's a rock the harbor fears.
It bleats in the crooked arm of time
spent until you see them now, but turn away forgetting.
Starvation carving its form
into even the most unwilling.

*   *   *

In hell, it is they who first come
forward to meet Ulysses, their transparent bodies
a story without comment: "Women workers: Mimi,
Tolstoy fan, my coworker
in iron bars, Mimi's sister,
mother of the burned kid."
And later, lyrical heartbreak, arc
of history: "Male workers: violinist,
conceited blonde,
singer at the furnace,
boy with mallet,
my fiancé,
his brother."
Elsewhere, here in the sound of the flypress, on the street
and opposing traffic, she places her malformed hands.
Their utility.
"Pity and mute indignation of neighbors."

Brothers, Sisters. Blank God.
A laying of but you will not touch me.

* * *

Elsewhere, here
in the sound of the flypress, on the street and opposing:
"We must make a new public investment."
Elsewhere,
the possibilities of fire and ice.
Feb. 16, 1991: Anthony C. Arguello, 51,
of blank shot his estranged
wife at blank
then used the gun on himself.
Under the moon's face, here
in the sound of the flypress,
on herself blank god turns
under the gun himself,
the possibilities of the moon's face
oh fire oh ice oh
pity and mute.

* * *

Not blank, not sleeping,
but helpless: the harbor
feeding its form,
the rock sunken god
mute and water, and the millions
turning a profile
toward your city. She's armless,
Venus of this,
faltering under their stare.
I could leave,
abandoning your body:

April 8, 1991: Martin Drew, 27,
shot and killed his estranged
But my feet in this mud
Nov. 11: Laytona Lynnet Logan
shot and turning the oh gun
    My body.

*   *   *

That year they were flagless
and she thought yes,
this is it, right here
that course, butterflies
pinned to white, a jet through an adulterer's
hour, skaters punctuating the flaming
    ROSE on the laborer's chest
and what after all still left.
    In the heartbreak of her year:
"The important thing is to be nothing."
Though what she had come to resemble then
was something entire.

*   *   *

That which disappears
and saith unto him: teacher
and saith unto her: touch me not,
sympathy and her object
not deferred but subject
to partage, light
and the integrity of a prism.

OUTSIDE GARDEN

RICHTER

Only machinery transcribes deceit,
the lie detector's penciled
hills and valleys wherein intention
is painted, the flat line of the heart
monitor, the end of god's finger. A camera
   returning each time to the face
of the face she wanted to be *I swear*
this time I'll make it right, love only you, etc.
The day gathering around that vow
corresponding accordingly: the air, true,
   clothes strung on the taut wire, true,
this shoe goes here, these papers, here,
these words, that telegram, here, here.
Though the car waits to take her some other where
(let her stay here for now). And travel—
   where is the woman of the last second? where
is she?—also true, past the neighborhood's lie
of order, the corn finishing in a field,
an anthem she thought she knew by heart,
silenced in the yellow grass. As if there's one gene for God
   and all the others for betrayal, this holy war
ends in the unseen, maskless and then the burning
she inhales, unbelieving. Until then, sleep, an airplane's
drone and she wakes up finally past evening,
past change, insect's season done, dinners called for,
   done and love: the miles of phone wire
thread tangibly in her veins so that she
must hold herself carefully, hovering as she is
over a new precipice, to see better from this distance the
flaming moth sleep has made of her.

INJURY

The true face of God is blank and sitting tightly
over a small globe in Michelangelo's Sistine Chapel.
A moment earlier he may have been stroking himself, his eyes
drawn back and riveted to an ant's slow travel across a wall.
   But now he is in the business of being God, the terror,
mostly horrified and gray, his hand in his mouth,
stuck between the *really* damned and the *really* saved
and far enough away not to be *really* related to the *holy*
   father, lolling a casual, puerile finger to Adam. I've spent
years loving the space between them but now I am gazing
at the real face of God who may have been touching something
truly, just truly but now he is in the industry of being God
   terribly, there is horror below the clouds it is gray
he is far away from his father. Every day should start with
this injury. Every day not really begun until something quite
sharp, without a thought for you but as matter, something
   to slice through, reaches bone and it hurts. *God why does*
it hurt,—the glass—at last, an easy answer and you settle down
to the business of hurting, tearing the curtain to stop
the blood, resting your head on your knee, calling for help.
   At last you've entered the canon of survivors,
industrialist of the common rag and dry bread and thoughts
so energetically away from the first idea, they become it.
It is winter. All you have to do is keep moving, shuffling
   your feet slowly across the yard, an eye out for the noon
sun. Under it, you think, you will never think again.

THE END IS AN ANIMAL

The hole the day digs for your feeling is opening now. Let it go.
Let it go or follow it in, kicking over the precipice—what does it
    matter?
It's not yours anymore. Puddles deepen in this sudden thaw, a
    hand
lifting—do you feel it?—from your mouth, breath stabilizing,
    you call *this*
the spirit of the matter? Nothing huge and old and incredibly
    wise is living
under the field somewhere. And what drifts against your throat
    sometimes—oh pity
it. Muttering weak God, patron of aneurysm, production lines,
    patron
of food banks and cool water, dear intelligence!

Dear Gnosis, most holy note: For weeks now, driving in my car,
attempts *to know* the story pouring from the announcer's mouth,
    I've felt
your bruised will sobbing from the periphery of the road. I swear
it was your soundless agony hurling from the tree line, to the
    houses'
small lights, and back. You passed through the car and I couldn't
touch you. Teacher, the body of God is a mass grave. In him
the souls are reeling and he is rocking them now in the grass and
    calling
us by name. Under the shifting clouds, he is rocking and calling
our names.

In the hole, birds thread straw through the eyes of your feeling.
She is the loneliest of girls, having forgiven even your
    abandonment.

She is the body keeping you from yourself, from God. She cringes
at your interrogations, she is a flesh lampshade, she is a million ID
tags, she is the sensation inside your bones. She is all that is true,
beautiful girl, taken into a coma by one after the other, into death
and still they won't leave her. And when you mumble *why God,*
    it is
her face, not his, that kisses your lids to sleep. Hear her whisper
    it's
not his fault.

SPRING

Somewhere in her breath my father's heart, her orphaned mother
lifting buckets. Scatter me in her breath. At this point
I was already (in her breath) far and away grown gone, I was a
   park
the city wrote across a map. Father heart, orphan mother.
I was that which none called back even as I slipped behind.

The depth of that place, the depth and striving disorder of veins
blocking, in her breath I learned this. The depth of that place,
over the phone wires for years, my mother's breath listening,
the struggling veins calling from a back room. Grown far
and gone away, the park assembled its waiting, leaves, snow,
   pages

where flowers stood up each when ordered by name. At this
   point
I am already outside her breath, the sluggish veins pumping
   slowly,
in cold, beyond orphancy. I learned at this point the depth
of that place, far away grown gone, my litter, in her breath
his heart assembling and a park behind gone green, grown away
from a map.

FALLOUT

The truth of the matter spreading out around them,
her dress dropping in the grass, a mushroom cloud
in the newly green sky. Why couldn't love be the end
of the world? It feels that way. Every time
it pinned her down, it was somewhere else she rose,
raising a hand to the face its light would not quit. So that she
woke in an artillery of bird song,
in October, birds unseen
in the tree outside, not a girl anymore,
not a woman, no just a *something* firming up on the periphery
of sleep. And the bird's frantic, autumn calls, the same
notes she fingers this most sincere wish by.

It's the pool,
though he'd swear to his face, *you you* Narcissus gave himself
completely to. The green water, trees and falling
safely now away, a place to be held up in. I think it is some
other where love would take us. And though the truest things
signal—wind through the grass, a ritual prayer threading a slow
incense through the heart of these words—see how I'm tethered
here, in sympathy for the seasons and blood, my kin; a bird
filled with the notion of winter who will not leave
so it may begin.

AVE VERUM CORPUS

It occurred in the spaces the community choir left in the new
    concert
hall. The body the composer was trying to make, I mean. In
    those
four minutes, hovering, but finally only *there* as they left,
    American
and amateur in the black clothes required. My people leaving
on crutches, in columns, single file, until their absence, the thing
he must have wanted, stark against the farthest sandalwood wall.
By comparison, the next, busy violin, gratuitous applause.

We'd been finally West, our figures in the old building's light
projecting from the cliff onto the ocean, unappeased. So far from
our bodies there, weren't we so far, I believed we might gladly
    touch
there, until I recalled how touch looked in the painting, the
    century's
comment on intimacy, our spotlight's hypodermic, a clarifying
    virus.
Gone, though we looked all through the museum for it. I'd
    known where
it was but even its wall was gone and I was afraid for the theft.

Between vision and love, too much beauty. A woman miscarrying
in a high hotel room and each time she opens her eyes again
the people in the building across the street, opening windows,
    smiling
out into the brick face, each time a new body and its morning.
And then the possibilities of the traffic jam, the bridge a harp
thick with not speaking. The American choir singing our body.

THE CAMERA'S EYE TURNED TO YOU AND THEN THE BEGINNING OF STATIC

Which is truth maybe,
or what the air collecting
resembles before it is made wind.
   A cricket all morning
trapped in here with me,
this listening threading
the long, nervous sound
to the day I can't be part
of. Not yet. Undeserving
but for the names my fingers
spell out on the flowered sheets.
Riding the cricket's chirr,
passenger, coward to all
but the silk string this
ties to the violin
legs, conducting. Only in the movies
are their real lives,
characters the viewers look
to, memorizing. Here is the man
who loves his wife
but can't be true. Here she is,
beautiful and betrayed,
her words the dancing ball
you follow across the screen,
to thine self be true and so it follows etc.
Here are his actions (call him J.)
the camera diagrams like a sentence,
too many declensions, parenthetical
arms, digressing, do you follow—
His life the city streets

you've walked losing
steadily the promises
the side roads offered—
a girl in a windowbox reading,
a stray, exclamatory arm
flung in the air, sketched
into your retina as reason enough?
His life the neuroses of present tense,
no breath signifying *start,* no exhale for *end.*
And she, the beautiful, sought for,
allowed also to begin and begin and begin.
Meanwhile my cricket clicks
on, clicks off, each
lapse into silence abolishing
plot, until it's an
orchestration of absence
I derive, turning sounds
over and over in my mouth,
this the baton lifted on cue.

ELEGY FOR ANNA KARENINA

In first person she falls neatly
under the train wheels,
without a backward glance
at him who writes her
descent the way the social contract
of those days held women:
in the dark room, a drawn curtain,
orgasm so many birds
over a graveyard.
See how she fulfills
a different kind of will,
freed from obligation and obliged
by her single wish to be
one *Anna,* dropping,
the cries too late
over the platform's stare,
freed from Tolstoy's intent
in a hissing of brakes.
And, yes, maybe it is *too bad,*
all outcome absorbed in her one act,
but it is short work she made
of his desire for her.
Anna, I have felt you
in me all my life,
but the day wants me in it
and the wind matters less,
now it is all I have.
The last seed pods
navigating the field
dissipate tragedy
in their easy

fluttering down.
Simply, I live on the inside
of a room whose walls
take the grain from my stare,
my windows toward the road
and the arriving.

HARVEST

There is something that would take our spirits here,
take it methodically, in passing grazes much as these birds today
whirling to and fro over the finished field,
worrying the animal we take measured steps toward daily,
because they know it is hunger they make carrion by.
Their low sweeping an indictment against what lives
too completely in the one arena, like the photograph
the Hopi will not honor for the soul it steals
through stasis. And though I pity you, scarecrow,
old man protecting the dirt between us,
I will not take my place beside you.

BELOVED

I wanted to betray here
   only this morning,
bald and trembling the front page
   child of this feeding
from a sergeant's beak.
   Patron of flowering slum, April slum,
American baby J.,
   sergeant patron feeding
what is lost, surveying
   betrayal trembling
only this morning.
   Confession:
      Elsie's gone.
Overheard, she's a sound too late to hear.
I won't love her or her baby
leadpoisoned in the sergeant's mouth.
The surface promise of music
and the worry underneath.
Where do they become the same?

2. Outside Garden

   Already a park to begin with,
a trainer running the naked,
   scared ones by voice alone,
light building a lattice
   then a cage across, around them
and you'll never be outside of me again.
   Migratory, boxed
here *in me*, birds, hunger songs,
   no place to hide but *through me*,

her hands quick to her face, his
    to her face, moot leaves, all
of it *with me,* the light
    bored now, lackey and used,
a holding tank, a firing wall,
    the back seat of our father's
used car. Days. Stretched
    in the grass, light, hum
-leisure of the finished why
    won't you help me I can't stand
your tai chi to some other where,
    grass, grass (in me). In between
their calling I heard the sound of rain
    but he turned it off, too, with a steel tool
(through me). Public, therefore, outsidedness,
his megaphone calling
a brick down on (with me) (in the unity of)
    the ones in clothes, the bars
wide enough to stick a finger through
    outside. Revelation.

3. Word

Want to say, you know, can we
get along? Can we get
Um, can we stop making it,
making hard   It's just not
it's not right I love—
I love every—
I'm not like they're
got to quit you know after all I mean
It's just not right   those people
never home again I mean we're all
stuck here for   let's you know
I love   I'm every   I'm not like
um want to say not right

not like they're not me
um know I mean stuck here
let's you know work   mean   out
stop hard making
to quit after
all I mean
never home again not like please
hard stuck I mean

4. *Beloved*

Not gone but gone on
     her child the girl taken
in the ruin,
     the sergeant's allies taking
both her and the child. In the ruins
(even here I'm among them
bewildered at the order of the old woman's garden)
     do you see her now, too natural to live
all ruined, the film ending in a hotel room,
     the one who reads, whom she has begun
to know by, shot in the hills,
     and Rome, the ruin ahead, where she and the child
will live, altered by?
              Not gone but gone on it came to me
what are you I can't betray you to the child
     coming of age between your legs,
what is lost resembling your face
     trying to laugh in the hotel room
(the pleasant empty dished, a pastel field on the wall)
     where betrayal ends.

THE WORLD AS MEDIATION

ONE PARABLE

Yesterday the cruel power of motors, today glass breaking in a
back room, how feels it, you wonder, the electric arm of God
sweeping through the phone wire? She has the inward eye of the
ecstatic, our Bernadette, sweetly, sweetly, "thinking of it as the
tender shelf that connects all that is decent in me to you, i.e.
you" singing, on the severe burns ward, under her breath, to you.
Under your breath she sings sweetly, half angel, half grass, all
feathers and lap, thinking of it, the tender shelf, singing your
breath. Kindness is utility. It rakes the field of grass:
Bernadette, her arms too full to give a single blade. Half angel,
half grass, she hovers beneath your breath, sweetly, thinking of
it, what connects, the tender shelf, what is decent singing on
the severe burns ward, in me to you, i.e. you.

PARABLE 2

Because when she dreamed the madonna always rode the donkey
and he and the governess walked ahead leading the way
through the mountains. Beautiful, the mountains, even
real, Indian Paint Brush the red word caught, even
Franco in his coffin
pulling a certain loyalty
here in her image civilization,
the gas disguising the shower,
the child renaming the bomb,
India disguising the woman washing her hair
in a dark stream. Oh what wouldn't give
was her best resistance, Bastille,
fallen snow, Berlin, hell even the Alamo
bleeds in this. Between war and marriage,
seduction offered from ugly American cars,
tuberculosis this year's cure,
the neon truth of the woman
voulez-
　vous
　danser
AVEC
moi
　?
the photographer's face gazing back at herself
from a mirror on the floor.
I did not choose to be blind, to see
only how they'd managed in their way
to turn her into a statue, to spraypaint
and piss on, late, much later, than then.
I wept for the governess,
her rope-burned hands, her casualty of skirt.
I loved him then but didn't know the words he sang
until I spoke them today, in the clear high bone of your cheek.

COVENANT

The thing you can't see
threading the chainsaw to the inside

of a churchbell, a dead
boy's grainy, newsprint face

pinned to the *that* you can't see
how these things happen

but there it is, small
body, blue shoe dangling

in a slurry of flowers. Something
in the day's voice is hissing

show me, somebody
is asking our daughter

to push back her private hair.
She shifts in the mandatory

blue, her dress the billowing
landscape you've seen

but can't name. Everything there
makes you feel ashamed but that's

not it. That rock is this world's bone.

CHALKTRACE

You have no choice but to be one
or the other here: gunshot, blossom,
India, freeway, the fixed autumn,
a child's eventual hair. History
of your cellwork shared
in the sculptor you heard the story of,
religion his métier and hugely,
the giant cross he'd just finished
in the foundry falling, cutting off the leg
of first his apprentice, and later,
years later, many crosses and abstract
stigmatas in red years later,
the body of the apprentice's son
flattened under—what? A red cross?
Oxidized, perfected stigmata,
a century's work but hugely
and finally, under the metal signature,
the body of?
      Batting the limited fly
of the 20th century, I speak to you now not as I would
but further away, therefore, more.

TO SLEEP

Meanwhile, distractions of the fan, a driving
rain, a redbird hitting up and up
against her window, bam, no it's more
like tuh. Tuh, tuh, tuh. Cardinalheart,
prettybird, little suicide attempt
each morning at her window,
there are no people here, only sleep,
versions of the bird she has listened
to all her life, its glistening wings
promising . . . Promising itself
a word she must discard now
being so near the nothing or all
that red muscle flexes for.
Oh take it back, pushy desire,
truth on a spit. Bird, wing please.
(wing) If the eye, plucketh,
if the hand, pluck, if the heart
plucketh plucketh plucketh
(wing, wing)
Thank you.

PARABLE 4

About then, this one regret,
"for which never happened
and which therefore exists."
The duck's wake seemed so welcoming
where you walked following a dream
of the one last teacher. He was weeks late
for the final, some absolute disaster
had occurred, huge winds, impossible
roads, etc. not an excuse
but everything you'd need to know there,
the only one left in the classroom:
Sirens. The wakes bleeding into each other,
the what of a helicopter, God,
you'd need to get better at this,
each event never happening eating
into the next. The tree's shadow
a convenient camouflage but to stay there?
Impossible not to take the stroller's smile,
to determine the river's single moment
of separation from itself but there you have it,
a canal, a body of water, its channel,
grass, wind.
And suddenly this kid with an orange boomerang,
taking off his shirt, pretending
it's a toy, that he can *throw it out*
and it will return to him!!
It missed him each time,
little hero, wandering wide
of his attempts—"It doesn't work"—
sadly, boy with an instrument,
(such freedom, the audience
cut loose, can't face)

failed at his feet.
He made me watch a moth,
my teacher,
winding up a staircase,
growing at each tier until
it was a man with wings
I'd thought I'd seen before,
face pressing the highest window's stare.

PARABLE 4B
(AGAINST THE OBJECTIVE CORRELATIVE)

Angel of death, then, flashing,
a black man, his huge white wings
flashing, a slow crossing back and forth the river
three women must perpetually
run dark water through the long hair of—
$\qquad\qquad\qquad\qquad$ This begins
where the story disintegrates
into your betrayals,
the factors no longer x, no longer
y, those freedoms, but father's infidelity,
history's trite, revolutionary fires
razing the city's skyline
in the teacher's act of description: "I don't know
the name for this but look hard, can you see it now,
how we are loved here, this metal
in my hand, its function (notice the teeth in its
maw) to keep the calf from feeding
so that sometimes, so hungry, the young,
it keeps trying until its muzzle is shredded,
and this in a domesticated animal."
But the instrument was in your hand.
Why didn't we bury it in flowers,
string it through with Christmas
lights and hang it at the local bar?
I could say I understand. I will not understand.
The high injustice of that sound, again,
in Primo Levi's *Survival in Auschwitz,*
a boy, in line to be gassed
and knowing so, meets his father
a few people ahead of him, the old man

crying at himself in the boy's face, the line
still slowly moving, the boy, suddenly stunned seeing
his father doesn't know his death,
spares him: "After the bath, father,"
(you can hear his gentleness) "then we will speak . . ."
There are no words in his version,
story occurring in the hair on the water,
impossibly long, women's faces never viewed,
the water-hair impossibly unclean.

PARABLE 5

On the outside, like you,
of the public garden, the well-kept secret
not held in my hand.

                  I saw today a face
in the duck pond that was never mine.
I wanted to love the face
but the water was a body
strewn with feathers.

Kindness is overfeeding the ducks today.
It is arranging
the flowers into a wall.

Promenading its muscle,
the world clenches—your feeling.

I'm trying to resist the way it works,
wire holding up the water's rock,
a border mending the flowers into a wall,
the circle I walk here
without a name.
I'm leaning against a tree,
its life taking place underground.

*   *   *

And then there was nothing
   and shadow straddled

the imaginary dirt unmaking
   love in the zero hour.

There was a password
   traced in the invisible

passage the summer birds
   erased as they flew.

No feather fell into her open hand,
   there, in the primary light

of blankness,
   in the absent stutter the neon wrote

in the streetless anathema where
   she failed to cry: unname me.

BARTÓK WINDOW

The tai chi of Saturday strains
in a string's worry.
This is the final park, isn't it,
the reverent pinching grace from the air?
The violin plays their biography,
best teacher, dissonance undoing
their desire for no body
and this is what they leave:
near spring, in plaid shirts,
a group of five making prayer
on the matted winter grass.

PARABLE 6

the true place is given
by chance but in the true
place, chance will lose
its enigmatic character.

YVES BONNEFOY

It could be elsewhere,
the day, the family, given her up
for good, the teacher holed up
and safe in his empty house.

                    Here she takes her life's work
back to the mud, her hands pounding
each sculpture down, *go, just go,*
the white fingers and torso of the lovers
separating, *not here you won't,*
can't—

                    Up to her thighs
in mud and still something won't
let her stop,
not until they are all there,
all the bodies,
there.

That's where it should have stopped,
her hands flatly
against the ambulance window,
already a done thing.

*   *   *

And name betrays us,
Saturday, maple vine, Camille Claudel.

The day shakes inside of this.

Two doves on a wire, head to head
(they must be mud)
a stillness bleating against
the symmetry to which
the other wires pretend
there in the treeline.
I know it could be elsewhere
(in this light, the leaf's vein
trembling in my hand)
I know it could be elsewhere
(threading its light
right through my hand)
Elsewhere, the mud birds,
the wire empty of flight.

THE WORLD AS MEDIATION

(for Ivan Lalic)

A birthmark, like it or not,
or a speedboat leaving in the beginning
of a newscast, no peace again
little planes speeding through
the emotional middle, everybody
fishing and a gun
casts, the news, and then peace
a little plain in the forest.
The poet has a young voice
and a scar from chin to temple.
A birthmark, like it or not,
even here, zero at day's end.
The forest is a color understood by water.
The words can't reach the peace.
We share an outside but not the same,
a willing, flawed god, subject to revision—
is the bear dead in Sarajevo or not?—
radio history a voice
outside of identity, the poet
both a nation with a Red Cross armband,
and a figure kneeling by the lake,
the birthscar pure color now.

SAME QUESTION

Not in the inversion and grace
of a Romance language, the woman beginning to believe
in form, filing nails, shaving herself into an island,
in English, in hesitation, the bald
equalities of location
without sex, (on her side in water an island, a reached
for), Impatiens in a pot, in the ground, a glass table,
grass, privacy, holding dirt, a cheek, rain
coming in jets, closer
wanting to speak the closer thing,
reach the easier thing, the telephone,
age, breathing, age and nothing done yet,
not easier but here,
the joyful current interrupted,
invitations, strangers a part of every day,
in English, how to know them, motors, dishes
clicking behind walls, the sad forks,
habitual, lifting, habitual sheets, habitual
twin owners, noise and habit, the forms
that name her, in English,
consolations of various verbs,
states of being easier than action
but harder to follow.

TRANSPARENCY

TRACTATUS FRANÇAISE

If I forgave myself,

(the rain glossing arrival

to the showers)

would the milestone again show the distance?

All travesties relatively the same

in the conventional syntax for prayer,

desire vs. duty, she subtracted

from he, God re:Us.

(oh reveal it now)

A child's shrapnel wounds

on television in Amsterdam,

a doctor's ministering I

would not have witnessed

in my country, but you see

how he thinks it's his *job*,

the sobbing cameraman,

that you *must not* look away

from the unnamed place for which

—her cries so near animal

it must be the end,—

a father readies her body now, crossing

her final feet, small crusader,

preparing the distance from here to

2.

There. To family resemblance, to "the place

where appreciation is possible

and connected to other members."

Who share the same place? I thought

it was the blank milestone I loved,

those erased gravestones the Resistance

wrote, and the villages too, Montpeyroux,

St. Jean de Fos, as indistinguishable as the distance

unrevealed between them. But it's in *believing*

there is a *here* I stumble, Wittgenstein.

Opposed by nature to cameras,

the shaved head

of a French girl, in 1944, whitened now

somewhere near here, calls outside

of resemblance to me, her tenure

to public suffering filling in

the numbers that are not the truth

3.

Alone, but companion to travel,

the *answer* revealing the distance

but not their single importance,

each digit heading the pages of the history

which even now is writing you.

The unnamed place at once here and not here,

even the milestones insistence on *there, there,*

a fervent version of here.

The gesture of the unknown

father arming his dead child for war, versus

an old philosopher dying foresworn,

counting at once on his fingers,

the words that assemble us.

WHITE

Nobody less sure and then less,

Calling the bugman, calling a doctor.

Third world animal, no place to speak of,

Until *now* wanted to name something.

Fiona or Chloe. Camille with silent l's.

Did it shape what matter was?

The virtual body,

The writer's frail brother, his fallen chest,

Terrible accident a main character now?

The difference between a slum and a ghetto:

Least sincere, best witness.

The building gutted, its *heart* taken out, fell inward.

A few old men crying to a horse near the end,

Music smearing the edges.

What wanted love but no form,

And something like music smearing the edges.

A clarity achieved sometimes in final diseases.

CHAFF

For things that suffer, only shape:

the oil left in the boat's wake, a violin

playing underneath its melody, the clean

fervor of a chair,

milk. The puzzle America invites

across a page's white surface.

Even the box in which the calf tends toward veal

owes you nothing,

and the tiny birds always darting at the edges of things.

Always on the verge of being,

the withheld tends toward

defiance on the one hand,

sorrow on the other.

Only last night the weight of it

told me I was blind and a liar.

All that I've lost,

naming things after the self I follow everywhere,

faced me quietly from a corner.

Almost a plea,

what is true as unwhite as milk,

the clean fervor of a chair.

RUSHING THE GATES OF EMPIRICAL GARDENS

The jury cloistered in a hotel room,

the jury by number. She gave it up, "poetry

obstructing the words that it invited . . ." For the most part,

I remember the kangaroo in the snow.

And little Walter's father sick and his brother dead.

Cloistered for the most part,

the kangaroo multiplying in the snowpane,

I try to remember "now undividedly concerned

with the total meaning of being human . . ."

Little Walter.

"As that meaning is learnable and expressible."

Kan-ga-roo.

Poverty is the first language,

mother of the doll heads

in the gutter on certain streets.

I was born, therefore, without a tongue,

only later finding vocation

in broken glass.

Illiteracy is best.

Its body a girl's, a question

unasked in a golden field.

She is withheld and thus crawling,

She wants out of this painting.

"But all the while the picture escaped notice"

passing in the rushed green

of the window I had so come to love

All was generous I could enter towns

handing out gifts I called my "understanding"

my ability to call myself, say, Walter,

without having ever seen much less smelled

Walter at all. Glory! At home in graffiti

and the asexual tendency of culottes

and Unitarian newsletters, "What I assumed"

threw bottles from a speedboat.

Wanting none the less than ALL

I clutched one day "my center" piecing

together in the staggered image on the camouflaged

fisherman's lure the NOTHING I was.

After that stealing openly and thus this parchment

from this place I know not at all.

I know they beat him and there were lots of them

and only one of him and that after he whispered

words of love on national television. I know that saints

die of hunger, in protest, in taxicabs, at desks in photographs,

that there is an opening

now, I can see it, in the ice,

but in the townships they are still afraid at the polls.

That the word must once and for all

become inseparable from the body.

"Total meaning . . . is learnable."

With my tongue. I will you always with my tongue.

AND ITS DISCONTENTS

The spirit is moving

the surface of the water

today, a school

of fish by light,

all mouth and forward

thrust, all mouth. What I can't see—

the body of a fish—and so

am drawn to light, blurring

the distinctions between in

-side and out, the mile

of surface light they wake,

lost now behind the trees.

Something mercenary promised.

The mouth of the withheld

open with laughter.

Saint Anthony witnessing to the caught,

strung things, emptied of motion

there on the dock. Old voices,

old stories. Shoal,

shoal, mouthing near the edge of a shallow.

But that was years ago.

What is retrieved, illusion,

god's finger a larger

form of water, manifest

most likely, in the tracings

the heart monitor or lie

detector would like to reveal. What is inside

spreading itself all over things,

the fishes light-plagued, staccato

jumps, the beginning

of a machine's war,

or a version of rainbow.

              Outside, debris,

week's end. The fish

too silver and other to be real

from the beginning. But the bird, this morning,

stunned by the window's half-truth,

flight passing from sight.

It stood and stared, not like *bird*,

but something shapeless, older and more

patient, for an hour until shadow

forced it back to name

then to motion then to—Neither instinct nor action!

A bird crooned is illusion,

is elsewhere, an effigy of time.

I live alone, have no neighbors

though my love gathers crumbs

in the next room

and the old caretaker bleeds

our well, burns the old grass.

My body knows us,

withering into its truth, a statue

in a public garden.

In time, the catastrophes weren't enough.

The believers burn again

in the family hour, the hurricane

a form of fan,

the body a word collapsed

under a flag.

Writing was in its origin

the voice of an absent person.

In one hand, a basket of fish,

in the other a ticket, or letter.

A little closer somehow.

PATRON

The airplane's drone wasn't elegy,

neither the saw's low song

to the future. I fell

under their province.

Tree's shadow on the lawn,

mine on this paper.

You're looming over something yourself,

don't you get it, though you

call it by the wrong names,

wife, for instance, or *cup*,

your six rare plants

swooning now by the Palm tree?

A mountain is a dessert and then,

there it is, a desert. And look at me,

I've lost my voice dreaming

of a plant that's newer than your face.

20,000 dollars or pleas, or gunshots

before you bleep, good citizen.

Your sorry detector trails

its ankles in the sand.

I owe you everything and still

you won't look behind this door.

I didn't want to grow up frightened

and laughing, plodding slowly

from the olive's word

to the prison of your inner eye,

but how I go, chasing the dusty animals,

raking the coins from your father's grave.

IN DEBT

You will be out

-side, and birds,

love this summer.

I've changed places

in the grass.

The water scared me,

both a spray of bullets

and a bird, white.

Americans walk toward me

but I married my maid.

Our child outlived the censors.

Tongue inside the word,

Luanna an all night carnival,

when she died

I went inside forever.

Painted sun on the walls.

Clouds got in.

Rain. Bees at eye level.

In the high desert, every plateau

   an altar, (its formation

or my inside calling?)

   the exterior you inhabit as I write,

is a virus that begins with swooning

   then liquid, then death. It's not your fault,

neither the medicine man's,

   agonizing on national TV,

a return to tribe. The end is in the ground,

   in the plateau's decline,

because nature created was the end

   of God, and only when the altar

finally crumbled and drifted

   down the Rio Grande, could we stand

here—free?—imitating

nothing at all. The end is in the body

and the body wants to end.

Asexual, open, faithful to

transformation, civilization's peg

-boy fucked into oblivion,

no face, no hands, nobody

to speak of, sacrificed

to a system of camps, Monsieur Cérébral,

nature meaning nothing without "you,"

open mouthed in the arboretum,

manifest destiny with an open prayer book.

I swear to you nothing

will suffer the insult of cleanliness

again, not here, everything

at eye level.

I am in the sun. A man is limping

by, twirling his cane.

We are out

    -side, and birds, love

with you this summer. No tribe,

    no cure.

THE SECULARIST

1. Grammar of Assent

So the world became me

and I became blind

                (as I wished)

light itself shrinking

into a word that spread

a long shadow across the Bureaus

where I signed my name.

Days and days of tangible bread,

functional shoes. Afternoons,

I teach them my language:

bread, cup, tool.

They want more,

love for example,

and *travel,* wind in grass

of fields I no longer see.

Evenings, the last light

no longer insistent

in the oil pools and leaves.

An overhead bulb caressing my set of dictionaries.

Even in the machine

there should be equality.

No part subordinate

to any other part

though in function and process

one body, one part

must of necessity be

subordinate to another.

But the desire for chaos had arisen:

all should be equal,

the subway's rotarian industry

canceling destination in each

stop of the train, the dull

exclamations of steeple and factory

punctuating as far as I could see.

Why should my heart be the piece

I can't form correctly

on the flypress? I keep trying,

losing whole days of wages.

Blind or not, the light's warmth

or lack thereof

finds me at the wheel.

Power failure.

Didn't make the rate.

In the utmost logic of exile,

all aims waste toward an elsewhere.

Didn't make the rate.

You know how much I used to like Plato.

Today I realized he lied.

This world is not a reflection of the ideal,

but of us who are filthy and die.

The tool forms them and makes a hole.

Not belonging to any place, any time, any love.

2. *Apology*

My son, my only,

    fed now and asleep,

exile stiffens into presence

    on the periphery

of the graveyard and headstone seller's

    functional, corner lot.

It was Christ

    -mas, rows of wreaths

punctuated the graves, rows

    and rows of consolation

and habit in evergreen

    and red ribbon. Oh elsewhere,

I could not go in. Couldn't pass

    the gate prohibiting dogs and bicycles,

couldn't stride past the seraphim,

    in. Standing by the ridiculous markers,

my breasts leaking milk, wanting to buy

    one. Plain gray. No name, no years,

wanting to plant the stone and have it finished.

    In the end, I couldn't love

the others nor the balloons

    someone dared among the wreaths

but turned back toward

    the God's dead son in the middle

of the cemetery, his mute suffering

    word of my word, flesh of my—

I do not lend my ashes

    to this ground.

The smoke rising above the city

    has absolutely nothing to forgive.

THE CONTEMPORARY POETRY SERIES

EDITED BY PAUL ZIMMER

Dannie Abse, *One-Legged on Ice*
Susan Astor, *Dame*
Gerald Barrax, *An Audience of One*
Tony Connor, *New and Selected Poems*
Franz Douskey, *Rowing Across the Dark*
Lynn Emanuel, *Hotel Fiesta*
John Engels, *Vivaldi in Early Fall*
John Engels, *Weather-Fear: New and Selected Poems, 1958–1982*
Brendan Galvin, *Atlantic Flyway*
Brendan Galvin, *Winter Oysters*
Michael Heffernan, *The Cry of Oliver Hardy*
Michael Heffernan, *To the Wreakers of Havoc*
Conrad Hilberry, *The Moon Seen as a Slice of Pineapple*
X. J. Kennedy, *Cross Ties*
Caroline Knox, *The House Party*
Gary Margolis, *The Day We Still Stand Here*
Michael Pettit, *American Light*
Bin Ramke, *White Monkeys*
J. W. Rivers, *Proud and on My Feet*
Laurie Sheck, *Amaranth*
Myra Sklarew, *The Science of Goodbyes*
Marcia Southwick, *The Night Won't Save Anyone*
Mary Swander, *Succession*
Bruce Weigl, *The Monkey Wars*
Paul Zarzyski, *The Make-Up of Ice*

THE CONTEMPORARY POETRY SERIES

EDITED BY BIN RAMKE

J. T. Barbarese, *New Science*
J. T. Barbarese, *Under the Blue Moon*
Scott Cairns, *Figures for the Ghost*
Scott Cairns, *The Translation of Babel*
Richard Chess, *Tekiah*
Richard Cole, *The Glass Children*
Martha Collins, *A History of a Small Life on a Windy Planet*

3586